1   Introduction

Shamanism is the oldest religion on the planet!

In terms of human existence, it predates current-day organized religions by thousands of years—European cave paintings and carvings showing a shaman date from the Paleolithic era. Graves of shamans 12,000-year-old and older have been discovered in Israel and the Czech Republic.

Shamans have played an essential role in defence of the psychic integrity of their community for thousands of years. Shamans are pre-eminently the anti-demonic champions; they combat demons and disease and black magicians. In a general way, it can be said that shamanism defends life, health, fertility [and] the world of "light," against death, diseases, sterility, disaster and the world of "darkness"... What is fundamental and universal is the shaman's struggle against what we could call the 'powers of evil. Shamans cannot foresee the future but can change the outcome. For example, shamans can find out where food or game is located, so the community or avert threats to the community. This is a vital difference between shamanism and divination.[1]

This book is part of the Shaman series, a broad introduction to shamans and shamanism. This book concentrates on reincarnation and the beliefs and rituals that surround the soul. This book is connected to The Shaman Podcast—Episode 2, Reincarnation.

The Reiki, Shamanism and essential loving mysticism are complementary to our:

- YouTube video series, "Reiki and Shamanism,"

- "The Shaman Podcast" on iTunes, Spotify, Google Podcasts, iHeart Radio, Stitcher, Tunine, Deezer and more.

Connect with our Private Facebook group to learn more about Reiki.

Subscribe to our newsletter to learn more about Reiki and Shamanism.

Enjoy.
Mark Ashford, MSc,
Usui Tibetan Reiki Master and Teacher
https://www.markaashford.com
            information@markaashford.com

---

[1] https://www.energy-shifter.com/shamanism-and-spiritual-techniques.html, "Shamanism, and Soul Retrieval - Spiritual House Cleansing."

2   Table of Contents

3   Table of Figures

Figure 1. Reincarnation. Image by Chris0223 from Pixabay

Figure 2. Keep calm...

4 Tibetan Book of the Dead.

Bardo—Tibetan—Bar does thos grol translates as: [2]

1. Bardo's "intermediate state," "transitional state," "in between state," and "liminal state," which is synonymous with the Sanskrit antarabhāva. Valdez: "Used loosely, the term 'Bardo' refers to the state of existence intermediate between two lives on earth." Valdez: "[The] concept arose soon after the Buddha's passing, with several earlier Buddhist groups accepting the existence of such an intermediate state, while other schools rejected it."

2. Thos grol: "liberation," which is synonymous with the Sanskrit word bodhi, "awakening," "understanding," "enlightenment," and synonymous with the term nirvana, "blowing out," "extinction," "the extinction of illusion."

3. In Tibetan Buddhism, Bardo is the central theme of the Bardo Thodollly Liberation Through Hearing During the Intermediate State or the Tibetan Book of the Dead

4.1 Origins.

In Tibetan tradition, the Bardo Thodol, Liberation Through Hearing During the Intermediate State — The Tibetan Book of the Dead was composed in the 8th century by Padmasambhava, written by his primary student, Yeshe Tsogyal, buried in the Gampo hills in central Tibet and subsequently discovered by a Tibetan terton[3], Karma Lingpa, in the 14th century.[4]

In some schools of Buddhism, Bardo, antarabhava, or chuu is an intermediate or liminal state between death and rebirth—reincarnation. Reincarnation into another life, as a different being, is the philosophical or religious concept that the non-physical essence of a living being starts a new life in another physical form or body after biological death. It is also called rebirth or transmigration.[5]

Bardo or Bardo Thodol is a concept which arose soon after the Buddha's passing, with several earlier Buddhist groups accepting the existence of such an intermediate state, while other schools rejected it.

In Tibetan Buddhism, Bardo is the central theme of the Bardo Thodol[6], literally Liberation Through Hearing During the Intermediate State; in the west, Bardo Thodol is known as the Tibetan Book of the Dead.[7] The Tibetan Book of the Dead is a Lamest book of counsel, probably influenced by Bon shamanism. The Tibetan text should guide one through the experiences of consciousness after death, in the Bardo, the interval between death and the next rebirth. The text also includes chapters on the signs of death and rituals to undertake when the end is closing in or has taken place.

---

[2] Wikipedia, "Bardo Thodol."
[3] "Terton."
[4] http://donlehmanjr.com/, "The Tibetan Book of the Dead.Pdf."
[5] Wikipedia, "Reincarnation."
[6] Britannica, "Bardo ThöDol Tibetan Buddhist Text."
[7] Wikipedia, "Bardo."

One standard error with the Tibetan Book of the dead is that it is not whispered into the dying person's ear! In Tibetan Buddhist practice, the Tibetan Book of the Dead is used during life by those who want to learn to visualize what will come after death.

After physical death, the tribal shaman, a psychopomp or soul-guide, accompanies the dead person's soul on its hard path during the forty-nine days of the intermediate state between death and rebirth.[8]

According to Tibetan tradition, after death and before one's next birth, when one's consciousness is not connected with a physical body, one experiences a variety of phenomena. These usually follow a particular sequence of degeneration from just after death, the most direct experiences of reality of which one is spiritually capable, and then proceeding to terrifying hallucinations that arise from the impulses of one's previous unskillful actions. For the prepared and appropriately trained individuals, the Bardo offers an excellent opportunity for liberation since transcendental insight may arise with the direct experience of reality; for others, it can become a place of danger as the karmically created hallucinations can impel one into a less than desirable rebirth.[9]

Symbolically, Bardo describes times when our usual way of life becomes suspended, as, for example, during a period of illness or a meditation retreat. Such times can prove fruitful for spiritual progress because external constraints diminish. However, they can also present challenges because our less skillful impulses may come to the foreground, just as in the sidpa Bardo.

The concept of antarabhava[10] , an intervening state between death and rebirth, was brought into Buddhism from the Vedic-Upanishadic philosophical tradition, which later developed into Hinduism.

From the records of ancient Buddhist schools, at least six different groups accepted the notion of an intermediate existence, antarabhava the Sarvastivada, Darstantika, Vatsiputriyas, Sammitiya, Purvasaila and late Mahisasaka. The first four are closely related schools. Opposing them was the Mahasamghika, early Mahisasaka, Theravada, Vibhajyavada and the Sariputra Abhidharma.

To the shaman, the world has three parts: sky and heavens, earth, and the lower regions or realms.

Each has distinctive spirits, many of which influence the world of humans, including souls, in crossing over. The upper gods (steng lha) live in the atmosphere and sky; in the middle realm, tsen (bar btsan) inhabit the earth; in the lower domain are the home of yoklu (g.yog klu), most notably snake-bodied beings called lu (klu naga), which live at the bottom of lakes, rivers, and wells and are reported to vast hoard stores of treasure. As all things have a spirit, the spirit's living in rocks and trees are called nyen (gnyan); they are often malicious, and Tibetans associate them with sickness and death.

Lu is believed to bring leprosy, so keeping them away from human habitations is essential. Sadak (sa bdag) (lords of the earth) are beings that live under the ground and are connected with agriculture. Tsen is a spirit that lives in the atmosphere and is believed to shoot arrows at humans who disturb them. These cause illness and death. Tsen appears as demonic figures with red skin,

---

[8] University of California Press eBook Collection, "The Spiritual Quest," (1982 - 2004).
[9] Wikipedia, "Bardo."
[10] https://www.wisdomlib.org, "Antarabhava, AntarāBhava 2 Definitions."

wearing helmets and riding over the mountains on red horses. Du (bdud, mara) were initially atmospheric spirits. Still, they came to be associated with the Buddhist demons called mara, led by their king (also named Mara), whose primary goal is to lead sentient beings into ignorance, thus perpetuating the vicious cycle of samsara.

After death, the shaman undertakes a journey to the intermediate world and, with the help of their helping spirits, seek the soul of the deceased and guide and encourage it to cross over fully, significantly if the wandering soul has been affecting the lives of living relatives or otherwise causing problems. Or has been interacting with the spirits in the intermediate realm. During the ritual, blocked energies are released, transformed, and healed so the soul can receive higher spiritual knowledge when crossing.

The shaman may also be asked to help souls and spirits cross over who had no connection to the living. The soul has not crossed over and connected itself to a living person. That connection is causing illness. Usually, the sick individual or their family members will ask a shaman to carry out a divination ceremony where the shaman will determine what is causing the illness. The next step is to act on the reason that has been uncovered. If a spirit has connected itself to the living, the shaman will perform another ceremony to help it detach and cross over.

The shaman may undertake spiritual battles and confront evil or dark spirits and souls to help a sick individual or to help the nature affecting them to cross over. The upper, middle and lower realms are also inhabited by the spirits of ancestors [of the sick person], and the shaman must understand them and may persuade them to help a soul in its current physical incarnation.

The antagonism between scientifically trained and those professing particular religions can be considered. There is often a little study of each other's accounts of religious and psychic phenomena, so books like those mentioned are often not known outside a narrow circle of experts or academic authorities. Yet Carol Zaleski's[11] book has already spawned a whole academic field of research into the phenomenology of "otherworldly realities"—there have been several international conferences to date—while Sogyal's[12] book is now used worldwide to help people who are nearing death prepare for their passing over. [13]

In Buddhism, some of the earliest references we have to "intermediate existence" are found in the Sarvastivadin text, the Mahavibhasa. For instance, the Mahavibhasa shows a "basic existence," an "intermediate existence," a "birth existence," and a "death existence."

The intermediate being who makes the passage in this way from one existence to the next is formed, like every living being, of the five aggregate skandhas[14]. Fact is shown because it cannot have any discontinuity in time and space between the place and moment of death and those of rebirth. Therefore, it must be that the two existences belonging to the same series are linked in time and space by an intermediate stage. The middle being is the Gandharva, which is as necessary for conception as the fecundity and union of the parents. The Antaraparinirvayin is an Anagamin who gets parinirvana during the intermediary existence. As for the heinous criminally

---

[11] Wikipedia, "Carol Zaleski."
[12] "Sogyal Rinpoche."
[13] Dr. Roger J. Woolger, "Beyond Death- Transition and the Afterlife."
[14] Wikipedia, "Skandha."

guilty of one of the five crimes without interval (Anantara), he passes in quite the same way by an intermediate existence at the end of which he is reborn necessarily in hell.[15]

What are an intermediate being and an intermediate existence? Intermediate existence, which inserts itself between existence at death and existence at birth, not having arrived at where it should go, cannot be said to be born. Between the end, the five skandhas of the moment of death—and arising, the five skandhas of the moment of rebirth—there is found an existence—a "body" of five skandhas—that goes to the place of renewal. This existence between two realms of rebirth (gati) is called an intermediate existence. The skandhas are referred to as heaps because they're merely collections of parts with no central core.

Skandha	Description
Form	Your physical body—traditionally, these are listed as the eyes, ears, nose, tongue, body, and mind.
Feeling	The sensations you experience in your body, including all pain and pleasure.
Perception	You have sense organs, and each of them has objected. Put them together—eye and light, nose and smell, etc.—and you have perception.
Mental	All your concepts and thoughts, from the most mundane to the most exquisite.
Consciousness	Simply put, this is your awareness of the previous skandhas.

4.2   Six Bardo States

These are transitional states within 49 days. The deceased's soul is transitioning to their next life, their rebirth. But Bardo refers to that state in which we have lost our old reality, which is no longer available.

Our idea of the strict dichotomy between existence and nonexistence makes death and impermanence painful. Knowing something beyond that dualism is paramount. At the moment of death, instead of being caught between the ideas of existence and nonexistence, instead of this crisis of having everything that matters to us taken away all at once, something else can open up entirely; we shift our attention to the nucleus of being, to present itself, experiencing itself.[16]

Without some way of managing this experience, this unsettling discontinuity punctuated by occasional disruptions to the very idea of our being, we never know if we will show up in the next moment as a Buddha or as a demon. We're like gods one moment, tasting the fruit of the kingdom and hungry ghosts the next, not even able to swallow it. How confusing—and how fantastic! This confusion is the raw material of wisdom. Our path is to find a presence in each of these experiences. In the Bardo case, when presence is the only real thing left, wisdom can be elusive if we search for security instead. It's no wonder religion becomes so poignant during times of crisis; suddenly, presence is all we are. Everything else recedes except what is right in front of us.

[15] "Bardo."
[16] Lionsroar.com, "The Four Points of Letting Go in the Bardo."

Recognizing this opens up the potential to experience life with an awareness of impermanence and the presence it illuminates.[17]

- Rupture: There is a total rupture in our who-I-am, and we are forced to undergo a tremendous and challenging transformation.

This is the Vajrayana awareness of successive deaths and rebirths, and it is the first essential point to understand: rupture. The more we learn to recognize this sense of disruption, the more willing and be able to let go of this notion of an inherent reality and allow that precious pot to slip out of our hands. Rupture takes place all the time, day to day and moment to moment; as soon as we see our life in terms of these successive deaths and rebirths, we dissolve the idea of a solid self-grasping onto an inherently real life. We start to see how conditional who-I-am-ness is, how even that does not provide a reliable ground upon which to stand.

- Emptying the Contrived Self:

This is shunyata[18], translated in various ways, most commonly as "emptiness." Still, there is no real correlation in our language, no single word or idea that can cover this ground of disrupted reality. Because "emptiness" in English has negative connotations, shunyata is sometimes translated as "voidness," "open spaciousness," and even "boundlessness"; Nyingmas[19] such as Longchenpa explained emptiness in favourable terms inextricably associated with presence, clarity, and compassion. But in death and birth, shunyata refers to a direct experience of disruption felt at the core of our being when there is no longer any use in manufacturing artificial security.[20]

- Recognition that our experience is based on dynamic, responsive presence.

Our goal is to learn to relax and how to do so and fall into the inherent peacefulness of not knowing what comes next. When we do—and if we do—everything changes. We are no longer slaves to primordial anxiety.

Experiencing a loss can be freeing. When we are free of all our psychological heaviness, the accumulated weight of our usual momentum, we know the raw presence that remains. To be a Buddhist is to dedicate our lives to abiding in that impermanent, empty, visceral presence. We can bear with greater ease those losses we know we will inevitably face because we identify with the thread of wakefulness we meet in all of them. And then perhaps, when death draws near, we can ease into the ground of being as we shed this skin, finally, let go of this body, and experience liberation—an undefended being in groundless space.[21]

Please See—Bardo, Wikipedia—https://en.wikipedia.org/wiki/Bardo

1. Kyenay Bardo—Skye gnas bar does, is the first Bardo of birth and life. This Bardo begins from conception until the last breath when the mind stream withdraws from the body.

---

[17] Ibid.
[18] www.rigpawiki.org, "Emptiness."
[19] "Nyingma Buddhism."
[20] Lionsroar.com, "The Four Points of Letting Go in the Bardo."
[21] Ibid.

2. Milam Bardo—rmi lam bar do is the second Bardo of the dream state. The Milam Bardo is a subset of the first Bardo. Dream Yoga develops practices to integrate the dream state into Buddhist sadhana.

3. Samten Bardo—bsam gtan bar does, is the third Bardo of meditation. This Bardo is only experienced by meditators, though individuals may have spontaneous experience of it. Samten Bardo is a subset of the Shinay Bardo.

4. Chikhai Bardo—'chi kha'i bar is the fourth Bardo of the moment of death. According to tradition, this Bardo is held to begin when the outer and inner signs presage that the onset of death is nigh and continues through the dissolution or transmutation of the Mahabhuta until the external and internal breath has been completed.

   This is the first of three intermediate states between lives in the Tibetan Book of the dead.

5. Chonyid Bardo—chos nyid bar do is the fifth Bardo of the luminosity of the true nature, which begins after the final "inner breath" Sanskrit: prana, Vayu; Tibetan: rlung. It is within this Bardo that visions and auditory phenomena occur. The Dzogchen teachings are the spontaneously manifesting Thodgal Tibetan: thod-rgyal visions.

   Concurrent with these visions is a welling of profound peace and pristine awareness. Sentient beings who have not practised during their lived experience and do not recognize the clear light at the moment of death is usually deluded throughout the fifth Bardo of luminosity.

   This is the second of three intermediate states between lives in the Tibetan Book of the dead.

6. Sidpa Bardo—srid pa bar does, is the sixth Bardo of becoming or transmigration. This Bardo endures until the inner breath begins in the new transmigrating form determined by the "karmic seeds" within the storehouse consciousness.

   This is the third of three intermediate states between lives in the Tibetan Book of the dead.

4.3 Bardo Thodol recognizes additional states

C. G. Jung's[22] psychological commentary on the Tibetan Book of the Dead first appeared in an English translation by R. F. C. Hull in the third revision. It expanded Evans-Wentz's edition of The Tibetan Book of the Dead. The commentary also appears in the Collected Works. Jung applied his extensive knowledge of eastern religion to craft an analysis aimed at a western audience unfamiliar with eastern religious tradition and Tibetan Buddhism.[23]

He does not attempt to directly correlate the content of the Bardo Thodol with rituals or dogma found in occidental religion. Still, he highlights karmic phenomena described on the Bardo plane

---

[22] Wikipedia, "Carl Jung."
[23] "Bardo Thodol."

and shows how they parallel unconscious contents, both personal and collective, encountered in the west, particularly in analytical psychology. [24]

Jung's comments should be taken strictly within the realm of psychology and not that of theology or metaphysics. Indeed, he warns repeatedly of the dangers for a western man in the wholesale adoption of eastern religious traditions such as yoga. [25]

Bardo Thodol—Tibetan Book of the Dead recognizes three other states.[26]

1. "Life," or ordinary waking consciousness;

2. "Dhyana" (meditation);

   In the oldest texts of Buddhism, dhyāna (Sanskrit) or jhāna (Pali) is the training of the mind, commonly translated as meditation, to withdraw the reason from the automatic responses to sense impressions, and leading to a "state of perfect equanimity and awareness (upekkhā-sati-parisuddhi)." Dhyana may have been the core practice of pre-sectarian Buddhism, combined with several related methods which lead to perfected mindfulness and detachment and are fully realized with the technique of dhyana.

3. "Dream" is the dream state during normal sleep.

---

[24] Ibid.
[25] Ibid.
[26] Ibid.

Figure 3. The Soul Always Knows. Photo by Ava Sol on Unsplash

Figure 4. What is the Soul?

5   What is Soul?

I n Modern English, the word "soul" is derived from Old English sáwol, sáwel, and was first attested in the 8th-century poem Beowulf v. 2820 and the Vespasian Psalter 77.50. It is cognate with other German and Baltic terms for the same idea, including Gothic saiwala, Old High German sêula, sêla, Old Saxon sêola, Old Low Franconian sêla, sîla, Old Norse sála and Lithuanian siela. A more profound etymology of the Germanic word is unclear.[27]

The original concept behind the Germanic root is thought to mean, "coming from or belonging to the sea (or lake)" because of the Germanic and pre-Celtic belief in souls emerging from and returning to sacred lakes, Old Saxon sêola (soul) compared to Old Saxon sêo (sea). [28]

5.1   A Definition

The word "soul" can refer to the Spirit of God. Or, if the person speaking to me does not want to refer to "God," just "Spirit." It exists in each individual; it is ever-existing, ever-conscious, ever-new bliss.

Identifying the Soul with the physical body becomes the individual's nature. References to "spiritual progress" or "soul evolution" use this definition because the soul, aware of its true identity as part of God, is already perfect. Souls only develop or progress because they go from identifying with their physical bodies to identifying with God. This can also be called the ego.

5.2   Dictionary Definition

Merriam-Webster Dictionary[29]

- the immaterial essence, animating principle, or actuating cause of an individual life

- the spiritual code embodied in human beings, all rational and spiritual beings, or the universe

- Capitalized, Christian Science: GOD sense

- a person's total self

- an active or essential part

- of a moving spirit: LEADER

- the moral and emotional nature of human beings

- the quality that arouses emotion and sentiment

---

[27] Wikipedia, "Soul."
[28] Ibid.
[29] Merriam-Webster Dictionary, "Definition of Soul by Merriam-Webster."

- spiritual or moral force: FERVOUR

5.3   Atman—Hinduism

Atman is a Sanskrit word that means inner self, spirit, or soul. In Hindu philosophy, especially in the Vedanta school of Hinduism, Atman is the first principle, the true self of an individual beyond identification with phenomena, the essence of an individual. To attain liberation (moksha), a human being must gain self-knowledge, realizing that one's true self is identical to the transcendent self-Brahman.

The six orthodox Hinduism schools believe that Atman (soul, self) exists in every being. This is a significant difference from the Buddhist doctrine of Anatta, which holds that there is no unchanging soul or self.

5.4   Theological Soul

The soul and the spirit are the two primary immaterial parts that Scripture ascribes to humanity.[30] The word spirit refers only to the intangible facet of society. Human beings have a spirit, but we are not spirits. However, the word's soul, and spirit, are often used interchangeably; the primary distinction between soul and spirit is that in men and women, the soul has animate life or is the seat of the senses, desires, affections, and appetites.

The soul, in many religious, philosophical, and mythological traditions, is the ethereal essence of a living being. The soul or psyche comprises the mental abilities of a living being: reason, character, feeling, consciousness, memory, perception, thinking, etc. Depending on the philosophical system, a soul can either be mortal or immortal.[31] The soul is alive, physically and eternally. The spirit can be active, as with believers (1 Peter 3:18), or dead, as unbelievers are (Colossians 2:13; Ephesians 2:4-5).

Believers in Jesus Christ and his role in salvation respond to the things that come from the Spirit of God, understanding and discerning them spiritually. The spirit allows us to connect, or not, with God. Our hearts relate to His Spirit, either accepting his promptings and conviction, proving that we belong to him (Romans 8:16) or resisting him and confirming that we do not have spiritual life (Acts 7:51).
The spirit is the element in humanity that allows us to have an intimate relationship with God. Whenever the word spirit is used, it refers to the immaterial part of humanity that "connects" with God, who himself is spirit (John 4:24).

Judaism and Christianity teach that only humans have immortal souls, although immortality is disputed within Judaism, and Plato may have influenced the concept of immortality.

The "origin of the soul" has provided a vexing question in Christianity. The major theories put forward include soul creationism, traducianism, and pre-existence. According to soul creationism, God creates each soul created directly, either at conception or at some later time. According to traducianism, the soul comes from the parents through the natural generation. According to the pre-existence theory, the soul exists before conception. There have been differing thoughts

---

[30] GotQuestions.org, "What Is the Difference between the Soul and Spirit of Man?."
[31] Wikipedia, "Soul."

regarding whether human embryos have souls from the source or whether there is a point between conception and birth where the fetus gains a soul, consciousness, and personhood. Stances in this question might play a role in judgments on the morality of abortion.[32]

The most basic meaning of "soul" is "life," there is no distinction between physical or eternal life. Jesus asks what it profits a man to gain the entire world and lose his soul, referring to his eternal life (Matthew 16:26). Both Old and New Testaments reiterate we are to love God completely, with the whole "soul" which refers to everything that is in us that makes us alive (Deuteronomy 6:4-5; Mark 12:30). Whenever the word "soul" is used, it can refer to the whole person, whether physically active or in the afterlife.

The soul is our source of absolute uniqueness, connecting you to your value and essence and the value and importance of every other living being. This is limiting; we will get back to that later.

---

[32] Ibid.

6   Where is the Soul in the Physical Body?

Debate on "where" the soul is in a physical body is a significant and disruptive discussion topic mostly because we do not have a suitable definition to recognize the soul if we are lucky enough or astute enough to find it!

- Descartes: The pineal gland is a tiny organ in the brain's centre that played an essential role in Descartes's philosophy. He regarded it as the principal seat of the soul and the place where all our thoughts are formed.[33]

- Leonardo da Vinci used his experience in anatomy to hypothesize that the soul was in the optic chiasm, near the third ventricle of the brain. His views were supported by observations of change in perception following disturbances to that area of the brain.[34]

- In De Anima (On the Soul), Aristotle suggests that the organs of the body are required for the soul to interact with. Unlike Plato, Aristotle believed the soul's existence was not separate from the human body. Thus the soul could not be immortal. Similarly to Plato, however, Aristotle believed the soul is composed of three parts: the vegetative, sensitive, and rational. Growth and reproduction result from the vegetative soul and are found in all organisms. The sensitive soul allows for sensation and movement in humans and animals. The third, the rational, is exclusive to humans and allows for rational thought.[35]

6.1   Ensoulment

After considering "where" the soul can be found in the body, how does it get there, and when does it arrive?

In religion, ensoulment is the moment a human being gains a soul.[36] [37] Some religions say that a soul is newly created within a developing child, and others, especially believes that belief in reincarnation[38], say that the soul is pre-existing and added at a particular stage of development.

In the time of Aristotle, it was widely believed that the human soul entered the forming body at 40 days (male embryos) or 90 days (female embryos), and quickening showed a soul. Other religious views are that ensoulment happens at the moment of conception; or when the child takes the first breath after being born; at the formation of the nervous system and brain; at the first brain activity (e.g., heartbeat); or when the fetus can survive independently of the uterus (viability).[39]

The concept is closely related to debates on the morality of abortion and the character of contraception. Religious beliefs that human life has an innate sacredness has motivated many

---

[33] Stanford Encyclopedia of Philosophy, "Descartes and the Pineal Gland."
[34] Wikipedia, "History of the Location of the Soul."
[35] Ibid.
[36] Wikipedia, "Ensoulment."
[37] "Reincarnation."
[38] http://healerofheartsandminds.com, "Reincarnation, Past Lives, Suffering and the Bible, a Shaman's Views."
[39] Wikipedia, "Ensoulment."

statements by spiritual leaders of various traditions over the years. However, the three matters are not precisely parallel, given that multiple figures have argued that some life without a soul, in various contexts, still has a moral worth that must be considered. [40]

6.2   Shamanic Soul

The Catholic theologian Thomas Aquinas[41]attributed "soul" the o the alter ego that only human souls are immortal. Other religions most notably Hinduism and Jainism hold that all living things from the smallest bacterium to the largest of mammals are there, souls themselves and have their physical representative, the body, in the world. The actual self is the soul. The body is simply a mechanism to experience the karma of that life. Thus, if we see a tiger, then a self-conscious identity or soul is living and a physical representative, the whole of the whole of the tiger, which is observable in the world. Some teach that even non-biological entities, such as rivers and mountains, possess souls. This belief is called animism.[42]

Animism is a significant part of the shamanic worldview and an understanding of what this world represents. Shamans often work by reaching a different level of consciousness or awareness that allows them to speak to the spirits of the natural world, who can then provide them with knowledge and information. Shamanism often relies pretty heavily on animistic ideas with most shamanistic practices, but not all but animism can exist without shamanism.

The soul is the principle of life, feeling, thought, and action in humans. In some religions, it is believed that when the person dies, although their body is no longer alive, their spirit or soul moves on to another world. The soul in religion is needed for reincarnation, which is apparent in Hinduism and Buddhism, where, when we die, our souls come back to take over the body of any living matter. Souls are not only clear in religion, but are also clear in philosophy.

---

[40] Ibid.
[41] Wikipedia, "Thomas Aquinas."
[42] "Soul."

7   What is Spirit?

The modern English word "spirit" comes from the Latin spiritus, but also "spirit, soul, courage, vigour," ultimately from a Proto-Indo-European language, the language is the most widely spoken language in the world. It is distinguished from the Latin anima, "soul" which also derives from an Indo-European root meaning "to breathe," earliest form *h2enh1-. In Greek, this distinction exists between pneuma, "breath, motile air, spirit," and "soul."[43]

The word "spirit" came into Middle English via Old French. The distinction between soul and spirit developed in the Abrahamic religions and the Arabic and Hebrew languages.

In folk belief, spirit is the vital principle or animating force within all living things. As far back as 1628 and 1633 respectively, both William Harvey and René Descartes speculated that somewhere within the body, in a special locality, there was a "vital spirit" or "vital force," which animated the whole bodily frame, such as the engine in a factory moves the machinery in it. Spirit has frequently been conceived of as a supernatural being, or non-physical entity; for example, a demon, ghost, fairy, or angel. In ancient Islamic terminology, however, a spirit, applies only to pure spirits, but not to other invisible creatures, such as jinn, demons and angels.[44]

7.1   Usage

The modern English word "spirit" comes from the Latin spiritus, but also "spirit, soul, courage, vigour," ultimately from a Proto-Indo-European.[45]

Usage[46]	Description[47]
Christian Theology	Can use the term "Spirit" to describe the Holy Spirit?
Christian Science	Christian Science uses "Spirit" as one of seven synonyms for God, as in: "Principle; Mind; Soul; Spirit; Life; Truth; Love,"
Latter-Day Saints	Latter-Day Saint prophet Joseph Smith Jr. taught that the concept of spirit as incorporeal or without substance was incorrect: "There is no such thing as immaterial matter. All spirit is matter, but it is finer, and can only be discerned by purer eyes." In Mormonism, unlike souls (often regarded as eternal and sometimes believed to pre-exist in the body) a spirit develops and grows as an integral aspect of a living being.
Various forms of Animism	Japan's Shinto and African traditional religion, focus on invisible beings that represent or connect with plants, animals, or landforms (kami): translators usually employ the English word "spirit" when trying to express the idea of such entities.
C. G. Jung	In a lecture delivered to the Literary Society of Augsburg, 20 October 1926, on the theme of "Nature and Spirit"

---

[43] "Spirit - Wikipedia."
[44] Ibid.
[45] Wikipedia, "Spirit."
[46] Ibid.
[47] Ibid.

Usage[46]	Description[47]
	The connection between spirit and life is one of those problems involving factors of such complexity that we have to be on our guard lest we ourselves get caught in the net of words in which we seek to ensnare these great enigmas. For how can we bring into the orbit of our thought those limitless complexities of life which we call "Spirit" or "Life" unless we clothe them in verbal concepts, themselves mere counters of the intellect? The mistrust of verbal concepts, inconvenient as it is, seeming to me to be very much in place in speaking of fundamentals. "Spirit" and "Life" are familiar enough words to us, ancient acquaintances in fact, pawns that for thousands of years have been pushed back and forth on the thinker's chessboard. The problem must have begun in the grey dawn of time, when someone discovered that the living breath which left the body of the dying man in the last death rattle meant more than just air in motion. It can scarcely be an accident onomatopoeic words like ruach (Hebrew), ruch (Arabic), roho (Swahili) mean "spirit" no less clearly than πνεύμα (pneuma, Greek) and spiritus (Latin).
Psychic research	"In all the publications of the Society for Psychical Research, the term 'spirit' stands for the personal stream of consciousness, whatever else it may ultimately be proved to imply or require" (James H. Hyslop, 1919).

7.2   Spirit in Christian Theology

The word "spirit" appears either alone or with other words in the Hebrew Bible, Old Testament and the New Testament. Combinations include expressions such as the "Holy Spirit," "Spirit of God," and in Christianity, "Spirit of Christ."[48]

For most Christian denominations, the Holy Spirit, or Holy Ghost, is the third person of the Trinity: The Triune God manifested as God the Father, God the Son, and God the Holy Spirit; each entity itself being God.[49]
The Christian expression of the Holy Spirit emphasizes the moral aspect of the meaning than say in Judaism and this trend has continued into the current period.

The Fruit of the Holy Spirit is a biblical term that sums up nine attributes of a person or community living in accord with the Holy Spirit, according to chapter 5 of the Epistle to the Galatians: "But the Fruit of the Spirit is love, joy, peace, patience, kindness, goodness, faithfulness, gentleness, and self-control."[50]

The soul and the spirit are connected, but separable, Hebrews 4:12. The soul is the essence of humanity's being; it is who we are. The spirit is the immaterial part of humanity that connects with God.[51]

---

[48] Wikipedia, "Holy Spirit."
[49] Ibid.
[50] Bibleinfo.com, "What Is the Fruit of the Spirit?."
[51] GotQuestions.org, "What Is the Difference between the Soul and Spirit of Man?."

Christian Theology and structured religious systems are strongly based on a set of codified and documented beliefs and teachings followers are expected to follow. The centralized authority and an organized, often very wealthy infrastructure accompany these theologies and contain a unique set of rituals, books, and processes for an adherent to follow. From earliest times, these centralized religions have been a centre of political and military power. Even in the 20th and 21st centuries, state entities with enormous economic and military capability continue to exist.

According to historian Oswald Spengler[52], a distinction between Spirit and Soul has been made by the West and earlier civilizations which influenced its development. The human spirit can be seen as the heavenly component of humans' nonmaterial makeup—the part that is impersonal or universal. [53]

Some Christians believe the Bible identifies humanity's three basic elements: spirit, soul, and body. They emphasize that the human spirit is the "real person," the very core of a person's being, the essential seat of their existence. When a person accepts Jesus Christ as their saviour, it is their human spirit that is transformed as they become "new creatures" in Jesus Christ. The soul, which is the seat of the will, mind and emotions, do not get converted but needs to be renewed daily through the recommended Christian disciplines such as prayer and reading the Bible. In Islam, Muslims are viewed as having their own spirits, but one that is one with God's spirit. For Spengler, the perception of unity this idea led to important for the emergence of the "consensus" that maintained harmony in Islamic culture, especially during the Golden Age of Islam. [54]

7.3   Spirit, Non-Theological Meaning

The human spirit is a component of human philosophy, psychology, art, and knowledge—the spiritual or mental part of humanity. While the term can be used with the same meaning as "human soul," human spirit is sometimes used to refer to the impersonal, universal or higher component of human nature in contrast to soul or psyche which can refer to the ego or lower element. The human spirit includes our intellect, emotions, fears, passions, and creativity.[55]

In the models of Daniel A. Helminiak[56] and Bernard Lonergan[57], human spirit is considered being the mental functions of awareness, insight, understanding, judgment and other reasoning powers. It is distinguished from the separate component of psyche which comprises the entities of emotion, images, memory and personality. [58]

Your spirit is a material part of you. It is non-physical and includes character, personality, and feelings. It is moulded by your experiences and your beliefs. Collectively, these combine to be the external spirit you show to your family, your work colleagues, and people at the gym. Your spirit influences your way of thinking, feeling, and behaving, especially if a peer group or required style of behaviour or action is required.

---

[52] Wikipeda, "Oswald Spengler."
[53] Wikipedia, "Human Spirit."
[54] Ibid.
[55] Ibid.
[56] Wikipedia, "Daniel A. Helminiak."
[57] Wikipedia, "Bernard Lonergan."
[58] Wikipedia, "Human Spirit."

New Age encompasses a very broad range of spiritual or religious beliefs which developed in the Western World during the 1970s. The New Age philosophy is non-unified and includes beliefs and practices from eastern and western religious traditions, as well as a holistic approach to health, motivational and positive psychology research. New Age is so broad because the general development of human understanding started to coalesce across an amazingly wide variety of human experience and empowered people to castoff organized religious structures and organizations. New agers, as they are called, don't limit their belief system to one particular doctrine.

Typically, the belief systems seen under the term New Age adopt a holistic form of divinity that includes, but is not limited to, the universe, including human beings, and contains a strong emphasis on the spiritual authority of the individual's self. This is accompanied by a common belief in a wide variety of semi-divine non-human entities, such as angels and masters, with whom humans can communicate, particularly through the form of channelling.

Although analytically often considered being religious, those involved typically prefer the designation of spiritual or Mind, Body, Spirit and rarely use the term New Age themselves. Many scholars of the subject refer to it as the New Age movement, although others contest this term and suggest that it is better seen as a milieu or zeitgeist.[59]

New Age has antecedents that stretch back to southern Europe in Late Antiquity—between the 3rd and eighth centuries AD. Following the Age of Enlightenment in 18th century Europe, new esoteric ideas developed in response to the development of scientific rationality. Scholars call this new esoteric trend occultism, and this occultism was a key factor in the worldview's development from which the New Age emerged.[60]

New Age literature often refers to benevolent non-human spirits with whom humans can communicate, particularly through the form of channelling. The belief system contains a strong focus on healing using forms of alternative medicine, which includes a strong connection to semi-divine non-human entities. New Age contains the notion that spirituality and science can be unified. As a result, New Age places Meditation alongside Quantum Physics.

---

[59] "New Age."
[60] Ibid.

Soul Loss

7.4   Shamanic Soul

The Catholic theologian Thomas Aquinas[61] attributed "soul" to all organisms but argued that only human souls are immortal. Other religions, most notably Hinduism and Jainism, hold that all living things from the smallest bacterium to the largest of mammals are the souls themselves and have their physical representative, the body, in the world. The actual self is the soul. The body is simply a mechanism to experience the karma of that life. Thus, if we see a tiger, then there is a self-conscious identity or soul living in it, and a physical representative of the whole body of the tiger, which is observable in the world. Some teach that even non-biological entities, such as rivers and mountains, possess souls. This belief is called animism.[62]

Animism is a major part of the shamanic worldview and an understanding of what this world represents. Shamans often work by being able to reach a different level of consciousness or awareness that allows them to speak to the spirits of the natural world, who can then provide them with knowledge and information. Shamanism often relies pretty heavily on animistic ideas with most shamanistic practices, but not all but animism can exist without shamanism.

From a shaman's perspective, all things are energy.

The movement, or the transmutation, of energy is part of the healing of a soul, but the soul is also energy in its own right. In soul loss healing, the shaman must first retrieve the individual's own energy, the parts of their soul that have become detached. The reason for the energy becoming detached usually revolves around major life changing disruptive events, violence, physical trauma such as an accident, which involves physical pain. The loss of a loved one may also cause soul loss because of emotional pain or stress. The shaman energetically removes energy that does not belong and fills the void with a mixture of the retrieved energy and divine energy.

Soul loss is very subtle and is dangerous. Few people realize it has happened, in a significant part because we are always "busy" and do not give ourselves time or devote the effort required to understand and detect this change in ourselves. When disconnection from the soul occurs.

Most of us do not know that we have disconnected from our soul and accept as normal a numbness and lack of meaning in our lives. Because we all belong to this culture, we all suffer from soul loss. It's an epidemic and blinds us from seeing the potential for joy and wholeness in ordinary life. When you hear from soul loss, you see familiar things in new ways so you can increase your joy in what you already have.

Figure 5. Soul Loss

---

[61] Wikipedia, "Thomas Aquinas."
[62] "Soul."

How does soul loss show up at the doctor's office: As a physician [Lissa Rankin, MD[63]] I've had years of experience diagnosing soul loss in my patients, but Western medicine has no framework for this kind of diagnosis, and as doctors, we're not taught to treat this kind of suffering, so we wind up mistreating it. What people suffering from soul loss need is the deep medicine of reconnection with the soul, but in our culture, we treat soul loss too superficially. We treat the chronic pain with pain medication. We treat the insomnia with sleeping pills. We treat the weight issues with diet and exercise. And most damagingly, we may label soul loss as mental illness, such as depression, and cover up the symptoms with psychiatric medications that may make things worse by slapping a Band-Aid on a wound that's not healing underneath the bandage. [Lissa Rankin, MD[64]]

Sometimes the soul needs space in order to heal, and this may require the courage to make some external changes in your life. Perhaps you need to switch careers in order to give the soul more room to breathe. Perhaps an unhealthy relationship is constricting the soul, and it's time to get into therapy, set boundaries, or even end things. Perhaps you need to find more people to love or move to a place that helps your soul come alive. [Lissa Rankin, MD[65]]

Perhaps you need to give your soul permission to engage in more creative activities. Such external changes may be part of the prescription for the inner doctor of your soul writes. But very often, this major life overhaul is unnecessary! Reconnecting to the soul allows you to find peace and happiness right where you are in ways that are much simpler and more profound than you might think. It's astounding to discover that you've had what you needed all along and have been looking in all the wrong places. Perhaps all that is needed is to see the life you're already living differently."

In folk belief, spirit is the vital principle or animating force within all living things. As far back as 1628 and 1633 respectively, both William Harvey and René Descartes speculated that somewhere within the body, in a special locality, there was a "vital spirit" or "vital force," which animated the whole bodily frame, such as the engine in a factory moves the machinery in it. Spirit has frequently been conceived of as a supernatural being, or non-physical entity; for example, a demon, ghost, fairy, or angel. In ancient Islamic terminology, however, a spirit, applies only to pure spirits, but not to other invisible creatures, such as jinn, demons and angels.[66]

The soul, in many religious, philosophical, and mythological traditions, is the incorporeal essence of a living being. Soul or psyche "to breathe" comprises the mental abilities of a living being: reason, character, feeling, consciousness, memory, perception, thinking, etc. Depending on the philosophical system, a soul can either be mortal or immortal.

Greek philosophers, such as Socrates, Plato, and Aristotle, understood that the soul must have a logical faculty, the exercise of which was the most divine of human actions. At his defence trial, Socrates even summarized his teaching as nothing other than an exhortation for his fellow Athenians to excel in matters of the psyche, since all bodily goods depend on such excellence.

7.5 Soul in Christian Theology

---

[63] Lissa Rankin https://lissarankin.com, "20 Diagnostic Signs That You're Suffering from Soul Loss."
[64] Ibid.
[65] Ibid.
[66] Wikipedia, "Spirit - Wikipedia."

The word "spirit" appears either alone or with other words, in the Hebrew Bible Old Testament and the New Testament. Combinations include expressions such as the "Holy Spirit," "Spirit of God," and in Christianity, "Spirit of Christ."

For most Christian denominations, the Holy Spirit, or Holy Ghost, is the third person of the Trinity: The Triune God manifested as God the Father, God the Son, and God the Holy Spirit; each entity itself being God.[67]

The Christian expression of the Holy Spirit emphasizes the moral aspect of the meaning than say in Judaism and this trend has continued into the current period.

The Fruit of the Holy Spirit is a biblical term that sums up nine attributes of a person or community living in accord with the Holy Spirit, according to chapter 5 of the Epistle to the Galatians: "But the Fruit of the Spirit is love, joy, peace, patience, kindness, goodness, faithfulness, gentleness, and self-control.[68]

Christian Theology and structured religious systems are strongly based on a set of codified and documented beliefs and teachings followers are expected to follow. Clergy and religious institutions have been established for worshippers and followers to engage with.

A centralized authority and an organized, often very wealthy infrastructure accompany these theologies and contain a unique set of rituals, books, and processes for an adherent to follow.

7.6   Soul In wider Non-Theological terms

New Age applies to a range of spiritual or religious beliefs and practices that developed in the Western World during the 1970s. Typically, the belief systems seen under the term New Age adopt a holistic form of divinity that includes, but is not limited to, the universe, including human beings, and contains a strong emphasis on the spiritual authority of the individual's self. This is accompanied by a common belief in a wide variety of semi-divine non-human entities, such as angels and masters, with whom humans can communicate, particularly through the form of channelling.

Although analytically often considered being religious, those involved typically prefer the designation of spiritual or Mind, Body, Spirit and rarely use the term New Age themselves. Many scholars of the subject refer to it as the New Age movement, although others contest this term and suggest that it is better seen as a milieu or zeitgeist.[69]

---

[67] "Holy Spirit."
[68] Bibleinfo.com, "What Is the Fruit of the Spirit?."
[69] Wikipedia, "New Age."

7.7   Signs of Soul Loss

To a shaman 'soul loss,' a loss of meaning, direction, vitality, mission, purpose, identity, and genuine connection; a deep unhappiness that unfortunately most of us consider as simply ordinary. The soul is our source of absolute uniqueness, a place within that connects you not only to your own value and essence, but to the value and essence of every other living being. What makes soul loss so subtle and dangerous is that very few people have realized that it has happened. Most of us do not know that we have disconnected from our soul and accept as normal a numbness and lack of meaning in our lives. [Lissa Rankin, MD[70]]

Because we all belong to this culture, we all suffer from soul loss. Soul loss is epidemic and blinds us from seeing the potential for joy and wholeness in ordinary life. When you heal from soul loss, you see familiar things in new ways so you can increase your joy in what you already have. [Lissa Rankin, MD[71]]

Diagnostic Signs that show soul loss: [Lissa Rankin, MD[72]]

#	Description
1	You feel you're not as good as other people.
2	You yearn to be of service, but you do not know what you have to contribute and why it matters.
3	You strive in vain for an impossible-to-achieve standard of perfection.
4	Your fears keep you from living large.
5	Your frequently worried that you're not good enough, smart enough, thin enough, young enough, [fill in the blank] enough.
6	You feel like a victim of circumstances that are beyond your control.
7	You feel like your daily life is meaningless and task-driven.
8	You often feel helpless, hopeless, or pessimistic.
9	You protect your heart with steel walls.
10	You often feel you don't really matter and your love doesn't make a difference.
11	You're always trying to fit in and belong, but you rarely feel you do.
12	You feel beaten down by the challenges you face in your life.
13	You suffer from a variety of vague, hard to treat physical symptoms, such as fatigue, chronic pain, weight gain or loss, insomnia, skin disorders, or gastrointestinal symptoms.
14	You struggle with being able to accept love and nurturing.
15	You feel depressed, anxious, or chronically worried.
16	You feel you're not appreciated enough.
17	You often judge others.
18	You frequently numb yourself with alcohol, drugs, sex, television, or excessive busyness.
19	You feel disappointed with life.
20	You've forgotten how to dream.

---

[70] https://lissarankin.com, "20 Diagnostic Signs That You're Suffering from Soul Loss."
[71] Ibid.
[72] Ibid.

Figure 6. Soul Loss

8   Soul Loss and the Retrieval of the Elemental Energies

In the Tibetan tradition, there is the notion of "soul loss." Although this is an imbalance of the elements, it is greater than the imbalances suffered in normal life. It is a question of degree. Soul loss is a profound loss of elemental qualities and a condition of extreme imbalance that usually, though not always, is caused by traumatic external situations and beings.[73]

We say that the soul can be stolen by malevolent beings of the eight classes which are described in section Eight Classes of Being, in this book.

These negative, non-physical external beings damage our capacity for positive human qualities.

This usually happens during a trauma such as emotional or physical abuse, an accident, loss of a loved one, assault, rape, incest, divorce, surgery, or wartime experiences. The soul part leaves as a protective mechanism. In indigenous cultures, the soul part is retrieved by a shaman shortly after the trauma. In our culture, people can go their entire lifetime without the soul part. [74]

Someone may also lose part of their soul by giving it to a loved one through a desire to share themselves with another. Sometimes, a soul part may be stolen. [75]

Psychologically, this phenomenon is understood in terms of dissociation, and it is a brilliant survival mechanism for the human psyche. The major characteristic of all dissociative phenomena involves a detachment from reality, rather than a loss of reality as in psychosis.[76]

What has been lost can be retrieved by the shaman through the practice and rituals of Soul Retrieval. The ritual is complicated and requires instruction and teaching by a qualified master.

The shaman first needs to speak to and understand the recipient of the soul retrieval. He or she needs to understand what is missing, what has been damaged, so that they may undertake the soul retrieval ritual. Some will call this a diagnosis.

During the ritual, the shaman will enter an altered state of consciousness, or ASC. This may be achieved by dance, rhythmic drumming, plant-based hallucinogens, or alcohol. However, not all shaman uses these techniques, each shaman is unique and uses different techniques to reach the state they need to soul journey.

During the soul journey, the Shaman will join with either a main helping spirit or a series of spirits that will aid in the search for the soul, which may be in more fragmented. At this point in the ritual, the shaman and helping spirts must determine the state of the soul and / or its fragments and what healing needs to be undertaken before it is given back to the recipient. It also needs to be determined if the souls or fragments are being held hostage by a spirit and what the intentions of that spirit are.

The shaman negotiates with the hostage taker in order to get back the soul or piece they are holding on to. A special, separate ritual may have to be completed in order to satisfy the hostage

---

[73] Tenzin Wangyal Rinpoche, "Soul Retrieval and Related Ideas."
[74] Theinnervoyage.com, "Soul Retrieval."
[75] Ibid.
[76] Wikipedia, "Dissociation Psychology."

taker. In some situations, a struggle may be undertaken by the shaman and they're helping spirits and the hostage taker to pull back the soul or otherwise free the soul.

In all the activity of searching and possibly struggling with a spirit, the shaman must protect his or her own spirit. Ensure it remains intact and is not damaged by the actions undertaken. The strength of the helping spirits and experience of the shaman in preforming soul retrieval is essential to the success of the ritual.

Once the shaman and their helping spirits have gathered the soul and any fragments and have healed them, they must be returned to the recipient. The traditional reintegration of the soul with the recipient's physical being is through breath. The shaman breathes hard at or on the recipient and matches the intensity, intending to send the soul back to them, and focusing on returning their light. The soul or soul fragments at this stage are like lost children being returned to their parent.

Then we support the client to integrate this extra energy, by first just allowing the energy to sink down into their bones and cells, which goes deeply into the recipient.

8.1   Element Retrieval

As with soul retrieval, the elemental energy of a recipient may be lost, stolen, or so seriously unbalanced, it may appear that a particular element is being taken away.
Sutra, Tantra, and the shamanic vehicles include practices to reconnect us to the positive qualities. This process is not just about having pleasant experiences; it is about connecting to deeper aspects of ourselves. Although ultimately, we need to go beyond the simplicity of positive and negative, until we actually do, positive qualities lead us closer to the experience of the base of existence, while negative qualities distract us and lead further into abstraction.[77]

When elemental qualities are lost, there is a flattening of experience, a loss of richness and resonance. This is like the experience of a broken heart. A man or woman loses a spouse or partner shockingly, is betrayed or abandoned, and he or she closes the heart. This is a familiar theme in novels and movies: the person can't love because of the fear of being hurt again. The same inner damage can happen when someone loses a child, is raped, witness's brutality, is subjected to brutality, goes through a war, is in a car accident, or loses a house—the catastrophes and calamities that fall upon us humans. The shock to the soul overwhelms it with fear, loss, or some other powerful emotion and, and the result is the loss of positive qualities, losing life force and vitality, losing joy and empathy. It may also result in physical frailty and losing sensory clarity.[78]

Regardless of whether losing elemental energy is sudden or occurs over time, or results from a traumatizing or dehumanizing environment, the damage to the energy of the elements and their balance in the recipient occurs. The cause is a negative spirit or spirits.

When we are physically weakened, our physical body is susceptible to bacterial and virus infections from bacteria and viruses. When we are psychically weakened, we are susceptible to the influences of negative non-physical beings.

---

[77] Tenzin Wangyal Rinpoche, "Tibetan Soul Retrieval."
[78] "Soul Retrieval and Related Ideas."

After an accident, for instance, an individual may experience lethargy, a loss of inspiration and creativity, or a loss of vigour. This condition may heal naturally, but if it doesn't, if fire element energy has been lost, it can become chronic. This may show up in work and in relationships, and may manifest in the body as an illness and in the mind as a disturbance in cognitive activity. The accident is the apparent physical cause of the loss, but the actual loss is caused by trauma or can come as the person is weakened and vulnerable to malevolent external beings. In either case, the damage is manifested in the soul.[79]

Element retrieval also refers to the overabundance of an element which causes spiritual imbalance. The shaman must soul journey to discover the source of the abundance and remove it, and, after removing it, the shaman must rebalance the elements and manage any damage by the time there was the overabundance of the element. If someone is too grounded because of the imbalance, the shaman must support the elements of Air and Space, for example.

---

[79] Ibid.

8.2 Blocked or closed Chakras.

Sanskrit name is used instead of plain English because the study of the chakra system as we know it in our modern Western culture originates mostly from the Hindu chakra system and yogic traditions from India.

The theory of the subtle body and its energy centres called cakras (or Padma's, ādhāras, laksyas, etc.) comes from the tradition of Tantrik Yoga, which flourished from 600 to 1300 CE, and is still alive today. In mature Tantrik Yoga (after the year 900), every one of the many branches of the tradition articulated a different chakra system, and some branches articulated over one.

Five-chakra systems, six-chakra systems, seven, nine, ten, fifteen, twenty-one, twenty-eight and more chakras are taught, depending on what text you're looking at. The seven—or, technically, 6 + 1 chakra system that Western yogis know about is just one of many, and it became dominant around the 16th century. The seven Chakra system Western yogis follow is that found in a Sanskrit text written by Pūrnānanda Yati. In 1577 he completed his text the Shat-chakra-Nippon—"Explanation of the six chakras."[80]

English sources present the chakra system as an existential fact, using descriptive language such as "the mūlādhāra chakra is at the base of the spine. It has four petals," and so on. [81]

But in most of the original Sanskrit sources, we are not being taught about the way things are, we are being given a specific yogic practice: we are to visualize a subtle object made of coloured light, shaped like a lotus or a spinning wheel, at a specific point in the body, and then activate mantric syllables in it, for a specific purpose. [82]

The texts are prescriptive—they tell what you ought to do to achieve a specific goal by mystical means. When the literal Sanskrit reads, in its elliptical fashion, "four-petalled lotus at the base of the body" we are supposed to understand. [83]

The seven Chakra system Western yogis follow is that found in a Sanskrit text written by Pūrnānanda Yati. In 1577 he completed his text the Shat-chakra-nirūpana—"Explanation of the six chakras."
In an earlier version of this post, I called the seven-chakra system, "late and somewhat atypical." But after a few days, I realized I was mistaken—a simpler version of the same 7-chakra system is found in a 13th-century post scriptural text called the Śāradā-tilaka ("Sarasvatī's Ornament"),

Chakra translates as "wheel." It is pronounced cha-kra with a hard "ch" like "ch" in a chair.

They are spinning energy centres in the body that lie along the body's main energy pathways or meridians. Each possessing its own colour and vibrational frequency, these wheels are the catalysts of consciousness and human function. The chakras on the lower part of our body are our instinctual side, the highest ones on our mental side.

---

[80] "The Real Truth about the Chakras," *UPLIFT* (blog), February 13, 2016, https://upliftconnect.com/truth-about-the-chakras/.
[81] "The Real Truth about the Chakras."
[82] "The Real Truth about the Chakras."
[83] "The Real Truth about the Chakras."

The chakras aren't like organs in the physical body; they aren't fixed facts we can study like doctors' study neural ganglia. The energy body is an extraordinarily fluid reality, as we should expect of anything non-physical and super sensuous. The energy body can present, experientially speaking, with many energy centres, depending on the person and the yogic practice they're performing.[84]

It is also worth noting that the essential and beneficial balance in our Chakras is something that changes from moment to moment, and from experience to experience. Balance is not static, and it is not taken for granted. What's in the balance today may not be tomorrow. Being able to recognize both balanced and unbalanced conditions is essential to maintaining health, vitality and good mental and physiological condition.

Being out of balance may be something other than a blockage in a Chakra. It can be depletion of our energy, especially when we are pushing ourselves more and more to be successful. We start to worry about the past and the future, neither of which we control. The past is complete and finished; the future is not just influenced by ourselves; it is influenced by others who may exercise their own free will.

Our well-being and realignment of our Chakras require rebalancing and healing by a Reiki Master.

The Chakras correspond to various aspects of the body's physical, psychological and spiritual state. Life force energy, also called Prana in Sanskrit and Chi in Chinese, flows through these centres and when there is an imbalance in one or more chakra inhibits this flow of energy, there is an imbalance in life—behavioural, emotional, physical, spiritual or psychological. Another way to look at Chakras is as regulators of the off the body's ability to heal physically and spiritually.

All chakras would contribute to our being. Our instincts would work together with our feelings and thinking. However, this is usually not the case. Some chakras are not open enough (being underactive), and to compensate, other chakras are overactive. The ideal state is where the chakras are balanced. [85]

When the Chakras are healthy and open, we too are healthy and open physically, emotionally, mentally and in our relationships with ourselves and others. When the Chakras are blocked by injury, illness, or disconnection from others, we refer to them as being "blocked," resulting in feelings of frustration, being stuck, and we experience a lack of vitality.

One thing not found in the Sanskrit texts is the linkage of Chakras to Phycological states. This is a Western innovation that started with Jung.

In humans, there are seven major chakras along the midline of the body from the base of the spine to the crown of the head and it is these energy centres that we deal with during a Reiki session. In animals there are 8 chakras, there is one between the shoulders of their front two legs, this chakra is known as the Brachial Chakra. Sometimes referred to as the Key Chakra.

---

[84] "The Real Truth about the Chakras."

[85] "Introduction to the Chakras," Eclectic Energies, accessed September 15, 2018, https://www.eclecticenergies.com/chakras/introduction.

It is the master chakra in that it directly affects all the other chakras. It also governs how the animal relates to and with humans. If the animal is unwilling to connect with humans, is behaving in a nervous, anxious or "skittish" manner, it may be a sign that this chakra is unbalanced.

The other seven chakras align in animals pretty much as they do in humans. The Root Chakra is at the tail, the Crown Chakra at the head, between the ears.

We will concentrate on the seven chakras in humans.

Because chakras can reflect imbalances in body, mind or spirit, learning how to read and rebalance one's own chakras is important to your own good health. A Reiki Energy Healer can be engaged to help with rebalancing but it is important to realize that the Healer also has seven chakras and they need to be imbalance within themselves to be completely effective and improve the health and life.

Once you can tune into the location of your 7 chakras, you become adept at opening chakras and develop intuitions about blockages. Think of opening and keeping the Chakras in moral order and ability to allow the flow of energy as a self-maintenance activity.

You can detect and solve problems as they arise and before they have serious consequences. In addition, you can locate old wounds and do the work needed to address them. In sum, through proper knowledge of chakras, healing can occur. We'll look at specific examples of this below.

8.3   Sushumna

Sushumna is the central channel of energy in the human body that runs from the base of the spine to the crown of the head and carries Kundalini energy, the primal evolutionary force within, upwards as it is awakened through the practice of Yoga and meditation.

Sushumna Nadi only opens and flows freely when Ida and Pingala nadis are balanced and clear, thus the purification of all three nadis are important for the overall health, wellness of the body and mind, and one can also experience spiritual growth.

Anahata said, "However, as a spiritualist, even though I enjoy all the technicalities of ancient wisdom and esoteric arts, I don't obsess over them. If our spiritual urge or intent is aligned to infinite expansion of awareness, potentials and consciousness, to love, to higher principles of freedom and balance for the highest good of all, then any sincere spiritual practice, be it yoga or plant spirit medicine, drum medicine or reiki, should support this process effectively.

Depending on the impact to us by events such as being betrayed by a lover, loss of a loved one or a parent, a physical accident, one or more of our chakras may have become blocked or restricted. If you sit quietly, eyes closed, warm, comfortable and breathing normally. No external distractions. Clear your mind let all distracting thoughts pass. Feel your quietness.

Rituals to unblock or remove restrictions in a recipient's chakras may be carried out to return the strength and vibrancy of the chakras affected. This also requires the shaman to engage in balancing and ensuring a clear flow of energy from the root to the crown chakra.

8.4   Divination

In traditional Tibetan culture, when people begin to suffer from this kind of condition, they ask for a divination. Divination is considered an important means to diagnose the source of energy disturbances and to show what can be done to heal those disturbances. Divination sometimes suggests the need for a soul retrieval. In other cases, even without divination, people may feel that a soul retrieval is warranted.[86]

---

[86] Rinpoche, "Soul Retrieval and Related Ideas."

Figure 7. Divination

Figure 8. Divination. Photo by Susanna Marsiglia on Unsplash

8.5   Eight Classes of Being

In Tibet, beings on each class listed below have characteristic appearance, temperaments, and how they relate to humans.

From: The Rigpa Shedra[87] and the Chinese Buddhist Encyclopedia[88]

Name	Tibetan Name	Description
Du	Bdud	The four maras (sometimes also translated as "demons") which create obstacles to practitioners on the spiritual path. It is important to understand that they have no inherent existence and are only created by the mind.
Rakshasa	Srin Po	a kind of malignant spirit that eats human flesh.
Mamo	Ma Mo	Wrathful feminine deities forming part of Ekadzati's entourage. The mamos are considered being among the main natural forces which may respond to human misconduct and environmental misuse by creating obstacles and disease.
Naga	Klu	Serpent Spirits live beneath the surface of the earth or in the water, and in trees or rocks, and are believed to be endowed with magical powers and wealth, as well as being responsible for certain types of illnesses (Wyl. klu'i nad) transmitted to humans.
Ging	Ging	Are minor deities who attend to the major deities in some wrathful mandalas. They appear as skeletons who beat a drum, wear a triangular pennant pinned in the middle of their hair, and ear ornaments that look like colourful fans.
Rahula	sgra gcan 'dzin	The Buddha's son, who also became the tenth of the Sixteen Arhats.
Tsen	btasan	Red spirits that haunt rocks are all male, the spirits of erring monks of earlier times. When they are subdued by a great practitioner, the Tsen often becomes the guardian of temples, shrines, and monasteries. Red offerings are made to them.
YakSha	gnod sbyin	The name of a broad class of nature spirits, usually benevolent, who are caretakers of the natural treasures hidden in the Earth and tree roots.

8.6   Four Levels of Guests

In a Shaman's ritual he/she considers the level of the guests invited to attend a ritual or ceremony, there are guidelines on how to relate to each.

Guest	Description

Figure 9. Divination

---

[87] Rigpa Wiki, "Eight Classes of Gods and Demons."
[88] Chinese Buddhist Encyclopedia, "Eight Classes of Gods and Demons."

Guest	Description
First Level	• Fully enlightened beings—powerful • Buddha's and Bodhisattvas • Free of Ignorance • They have perfected the five wisdoms • We do not control these guests • We ask for their blessings
Second Level	• Not fully enlightened but powerful • From the god realm, they make up the retinue of the major deities' guardians and dharma protectors • They may be from the realm of existence. Such as Angels. • Beings representing the planets and celestial bodies • Second-level guests help with healing. • We treat them with respect and honour them
Third Level	• Beings we have karmic connections with • Karmic connections can mean friends and also enemies—in this lifetime and in past existence. • A connection may also mean something that has to be completed. It could be a duty or obligation to another spirit, by the spirit that is in us. This obligation is often referred to as a Karmic Debt.
Fourth Level	• Guests of compassion • They are weaker than we are. They can benefit from our help. • In the BON shamanic tradition, it is important to develop compassion as a foundation for our practice.

8.7   Making an offering to the Guests

In all the religious traditions of Tibet, offerings are made to spiritual, non-physical beings.

The Mandala offering is foundational to Bon and four schools of Tibetan Buddhism and is made to the first and second level quests.

Other offerings for specific rituals may be Torma, Alcohol, texts, prayers. These can be especially long prayers or mantras, jewels, and precious stones. Also, acceptable is leftover food, or if food is not prepared or nothing left over, use of the mind to prepare and gift an imaginary offering is also acceptable.

While we prepare offerings for an important ritual, such as soul retrieval or healing, we should also not forget to make offerings when everything is going well. Maintaining health, harmony, love and happiness are important things in our lives. Preparing offerings to sustain spirits and our happy state is important. We do not want blockages to appear. We want to ensure we prevent obstacles from manifesting that may block us tomorrow. If nothing more, we are honouring our protectors and guides.

8.8   Chang-Bu Offering

It is a simple offering made of flour and water. It is called Chang-Bu or a fingerprint, Torma.

A shaman may make and use it, but this can also be made by yourself.

Mae, the dough so that is not too wet, it must not be sticky. Think of toothpaste, that consistency is an excellent guide for the consistency of the Torma. If you are male, lightly oil the right hand, if female, oil the left hand.

Roll the dough until it is a fat roll.

Press the dough into the palm of the oiled hand sufficiently hard that the tough will take on all the ridges, seams, and channels of the skin. Make sure the palm is covered, as well as the fingers and thumb. The five fingers and thumbs represent the five elements. We want to capture the creases of the fingers where they flex and bend.

Touch the dough to any part of the body that needs healing. This draws spiritual attention to that spot; prana follows the attention since mind and prana always move together. With the attention on a single part of the body, sensation in that part increases.

We can experience this by touching any place on our bodies and putting our attention there. When this is done with the Chang bu, we use our imagination to draw the illness, trauma, or negativity into the dough.

Try to feel a release in that area of the body. Move the Torma to another part of the body that needs healing. When we have finished, we have a substantial symbol of our illnesses, one that is energetically connected to us; this is offered to the third and fourth guests, the beings who may cause and maintaining the illness.

The intent behind the ritual is not only to remove the influence of the spirit from the body but also to give the spirit something, which is done through the offering. What is given has some of the energetic properties of the illness, but it is now in a purer form that will nourish and satisfy the spirit. When it accepts the offering, it leaves the person whom it has afflicted.

After the ritual is finished, the offering is taken outside and thrown in the direction opposite the individual's birth year sign, the direction, it is believed, in which the negative force is most likely to originate. (If you don't know your sign, refer to the chart at the end of this book.)

Traditionally, after a ritual like this, we look for a dream that signifies success, such as a dream of insects, animals, liquid, or other beings or negative substances coming out of the body.

9   Out of Body Experience—OBE

An Out-of-Body Experience (OBE or sometimes OOBE) is an occurrence in which a person experiences the world from a location outside their physical body. An OBE is autoscopy literally "seeing self," although the term autoscopy more commonly refers to the pathological condition of seeing a second self, or doppelgänger.[89]

The term out-of-body experience was introduced in 1943 by G. N. M. Tyrrell in his book Apparitions [1953][90], and was adopted by researchers such as Celia Green[91] and Robert Monroe[92] as an alternative to believe-centric labels such as "astral projection" or "spirit walking." OBEs can be induced by traumatic brain injuries, sensory deprivation, near-death experiences, dissociative and psychedelic drugs, dehydration, sleep disorders and dreaming and electrical stimulation of the brain, among others. OBE may be deliberately induced by some people using techniques they have learned and practised.

It is estimated one in ten people have an OBE once, or more commonly, several times in their life. Out of body experiences are differentiated from astral projections by understanding the former experiences to be involuntary, while the latter are considered being deliberately initiated and controllable.

The term Astral Projection refers to information meant for only the select few who have special knowledge or interest. Today, there are internet sites offering techniques and strategies that can be learned, so that astral projection sessions are possible frequently. To differentiate Astral Projection from Out of Body Experience, out-of-body experience "OBE" or "OOBE" is a more neutral term to describe the sensation of feeling as if consciousness, or the self, is located somewhere other than where the body is physically located.

Neuroscientists and psychologists regard OBEs as dissociative experiences arising from different psychological and neurological factors. Some psychologists view OBEs as simply hallucination in which the mind appears to experience the world from a perspective other than the usual physical body. Often the other location it experiences the world from the ceiling, in the corner of a room. Work has been undertaken to explore whether people having OBEs have any psychological characteristics that would account for such experiences.

There are some scientific experiments in which the person having the out-of-body experience seems to actually perceive distant events or targets, as if their consciousness is truly in that distant location.

The most famous application of this aspect is Remote Viewing[93] [94] promoted and experimented with the US Military and the CIA as part of their intelligence-gathering process. Much of the research into remote viewing was conducted at Stanford University in California.

---

89 Wikipedia, "Out-of-Body Experience."
90 H H Price G N M Tyrrell, "Apparitions 1953.Pdf."
91 Wikipedia, "Celia Green.Pdf."
92 "Robert Monroe.Pdf."
93 wanttoknow.info, "Remote Viewing.Pdf."
94 Wikipedia, "Remote Viewing.Pdf."

An intermediate position between the two extreme interpretations—true re-localization of the mind vs. mere hallucination—is that the OBE is a powerful altered state of consciousness which both induce a subjective impression of mind-body separation, and enhances the person's clairvoyant psi capacities.

9.1   Benefits of OBE

The tantrics mastered lucid OBE and dream states to overcome the fear of death by learning that we are not our "bodies." They also discovered that the physical body can experience deep healing during OBEs—the mind can be tough on the body. And rather than losing time to practise meditation during sleep, yogis continued working through the night while the body rested.[95]

Some athletes learn lucid dreaming to practise and visualize their game. By working in a dream or out-of-body, not only do they visualize, they have a "felt sense" of their practice, and can actually gain the muscle memory for winning habits. Others benefit from the opportunity to explore past lives as well as sped up personal development.[96]

9.2   Types of OBE

OBEs are a subject within a wide range of pseudosciences and New Age practices:

- Astral projection, in which a person's soul or spirit purportedly travels outside their body or even to a different plane of existence, and remains attached to their body only through an imagined "silver cord."

- Transcendental Meditation can bring about this effect through such practices as "yogic flying."

- Scientology uses some practices claiming to bring the "thetan" (spirit) outside the body and mind which is claimed to be the ideal state for more effective "auditing."

- Claimed alien abductions and near-death experiences often involve imagined or claimed out-of-body experiences

- Sensory deprivation or "float tanks," a popular New Age practice, seeks to induce feelings of floating outside one's own body.

- Sometimes, you just daydream a bit, and follow your fantasy with a powerful imagination, and then accidentally walk into your room in your daydream, and "whoa!" that's me over there on the bed! Woo!

9.3   Astral Projection

There are dozens of methods to learn conscious OBE and astral projection. There are two approaches—one is to keep the mind awake while the body falls asleep. It's tricky—the mind

---

[95] Gaia, "What Is Astral Projection? An Astral Projecting Guide.Pdf."
[96] Ibid.

wants to do what the body is doing. The goal is to take the body into deeper and deeper states of relaxation without drifting into unconsciousness. Yoga Nidra is one method. Once the body enters sleep state, practitioners simply "roll" out of their physical form.[97]

Ancient yogis would tie two frogs together before sleep. Once tied, the frogs would continuously croak—a yogi would use the sound to anchor awareness as the body drifted into sleep, and either leave the body, or enter lucid dream states. If, during a dream, the yogi could no longer hear the frogs, he/she knew lucidity had been lost, and could "wake" again within the dream.[98]

---

[97] Ibid.
[98] Ibid.

Figure 11. Near Death Experience may bring you to someone you know who has passed over.

10   Near-Death Experience—NDE

A near-death experience may refer to anything experienced during clinical death and subsequent recovery.

A typical NDE involves someone recounting how they plunged into darkness and then seeing a bright light. Sometimes the light appears to be at the end of a tunnel. Next, they recall a field of flowers and a figure in white who spoke to them about their future. Suddenly they come to, or aware of their surroundings and they are lying on an operating table with doctors hovering over them, frantically trying to restart their stopped heart.

Nobody really knows what NDEs are, or how and why they occur, though there are widely ranging opinions. Those who believe in the metaphysical think that during an NDE, a seriously ill or injured person's soul leaves the physical body and journeys to the entrance of the afterlife. There, for whatever reason, he or she is turned away and sent back to resume earthly life—sometimes with a newfound insight about life's purpose.[99]

The NDE usually implies a spiritual ordeal, such as an out-of-body experience, and is often cited by believers as "evidence" for the existence of an afterlife. In the broadest sense of the term, a near-death experience may be brought about by coma, serious accident, dreaming, drugs, stress, surgery, seizures, sudden oxygen deprivation, brain stimulation, or orgasm. Around 3 percent of Americans report experiencing some type of NDE.[100]

There are no "research diagnostic criteria" for NDE as there are for other psychiatric phenomena. Researchers frequently find themselves in disagreement whether what has been collected makes up a NDE, and struggle to ascribe causal factors to any experience.[101]

Almost all visionaries, mystics, journeyers and NDE survivors state their visions are, without question, of actual places or worlds, and though the worlds they experience are clearly not physical but they are real and tangible. NDE survivors have invariably reported talking to deceased loved ones, people they have been especially close to, and a godlike entity.

From a scientific point of view, there is no research, and diagnostic criteria that can be applied. The NDE experience requires considerable stress and trauma, to the point of death. Where the tipping point between death and returning and being able to report an NDE is unknown. This upsets the materialist who states there is only one reality, this one. To be accepting, the materialist must recognize assumptions of one-dimensional reality are untrue.

When Aristotle, following his master Plato, tried to summarize the knowledge of his day, AND after writing the physics, he had to add another volume, "beyond" (meta) the realm of physics, which in Greek became the metaphysics.

Plato had already designated a Metaxy, or intermediary world, of subtle spiritual forms that were not physical. Indeed, according to the eminent Indian scholar Ananda K. Coomeraswamy, Plato had already been influenced by the teachings of ancient India, for we find Plato's idea clearly expressed in the Hindu Upanishads:

---

[99] HowStuffWorks, "What Is Going on during a near-Death Experience?."
[100] RationalWiki, "Near-Death Experience."
[101] Ibid.

There are two states for man—the state in this world and the state in the next; there is also a third state, the state intermediate between these two, which can be likened to the dream [state]. While in the intermediate state, a man experiences both the other states, that of this world and that in the next; and the manner whereof is: when he dies he lives only in the subtle body, on which are left the impressions samskaras, Skt. Of his past deeds, and of those impressions is he aware, illumined as they are by the light of the Transcendent Self Atman.

Physicians and neuroscientists who've searched for a less mystical explanation for NDEs suspect their hallucinations, somehow caused by the process of the dying brain shutting down. Over the years, some have theorized that NDEs result when the brain is deprived of oxygen, or when a mysterious, yet-unverified chemical binds itself to neurons to protect them from that deprivation. Still others think that the brain's impending shutdown triggers a flood of euphoria-causing endorphins, or electrical discharges in the hippocampus, the brain area involved in memory, while others think the state is caused by the side effects of anesthesia or medications.[102]

So why include Near-Death Experiences in a book on Reincarnation?

One definition of NDE is: "A sensation or vision, as of the afterlife, reported by a person who has come close to death."[103]

Are we looking at when a soul passes over into the intermediate, non-physical realm from where they will reincarnate into the next life but returns to their physical body, their physical container houses the soul, and allows it to interact with the physical world?
If the physical body the soul left cannot function, it is truly dead, the soul must continue to cross over, walk into the light so to speak, and remain there before reincarnating to a new physical form or be trapped in a state of limbo, neither able to return to their body, or fully cross over.

Several reasons have been postulated for the reluctance to cross over. The insubstantial, non-physical world may terrify after being in the physical. A powerful attachment to a still living person may be another reason, an obsessive connection with tasks or a style of living in the physical world. Outright fear or reluctance to cross over because of the unknown of what will happen next.

Are these the souls the shaman encounters when soul journeying in order to help the soul cross over? Are the souls that attach themselves to the living doing so in to continue living in the physical world? Are they attempting to displace the soul inhabiting a physical body so that they can do this? Are their attempts at attaching or displacing an incumbent soul what is causing injury to the living and which the shaman resolves?

When a shaman performs a soul retrieval is he or she was gathering a wandering soul who is in this limbo state because they left their physical body and lost their will to return to it, or, perhaps the souls do not know how to reintegrate themselves with their physical body and continue their life?

---

[102] HowStuffWorks, "What Is Going on during a near-Death Experience?."
[103] Dictionary.com, "Near-Death Experience | Definition of near-Death Experience."

Figure 12. Altered State of Consciousness

11   Altered States of Consciousness

The Catholic theologian Thomas Aquinas[104] attributed "soul" to all organisms but argued that only human souls are immortal. Other religions, most notably Hinduism and Jainism hold that all living things from the smallest bacterium to the largest of mammals are the souls themselves and have their physical representative, the body, in the world. The actual self is the soul. The body is simply a mechanism to experience the karma of that life. Thus, if we see a tiger, then there is a self-conscious identity or soul living in it, and a physical representative of the whole body of the tiger, which is observable in the world. Some teach that even non-biological entities, such as rivers and mountains, possess souls. This belief is called animism.[105]

Animism is a major part of the shamanic worldview and an understanding of what this world represents. Shamans often work by being able to reach a different level of consciousness or awareness that allows them to speak to the spirits of the natural world, who can then provide them with knowledge and information. Shamanism often relies pretty heavily on animistic ideas with most shamanistic practices, but not all but animism can exist without shamanism.

Altered States of Consciousness include changes in both the content and functioning of the consciousness, usually experienced by an individual and observed by others watching him. The term "state" is not to be trivialized but denotes the states or stages of behaviour through which the individual progresses. Frequently people in these states appear to be in a sheeplike condition commonly referred to as a trance.[106]

A shaman learns and trains how to control their state of consciousness at will. This is necessary because they deal with spirits, of all types. They are energy and the shaman must engage with them in their domain, as energy in their own right.

Shamanic consciousness permits a shaman to view their surroundings as Non-Ordinary Reality— NOR. While the shaman is aware of what we call everyday reality, i.e., the world of humankind, he/she is also engaged with the abstract world of Nature and natural energies as well as what we call spirit. This level of intense consciousness brings awareness to all worlds, or realities of the upper, middle, and lower world simultaneously.

The Lower World is a world of energy, raw and full of dynamic potential. It is beneath us in the Judeo-Christian belief system. It would be Hell, but in shamanic terms, it is not. It is a world of animal, plant and echoes of matter's origin. Journeys in the Lower World are often associated with animal guides, power animals, discussions with trees, forests, mountain ranges, continents, etc. lower world is where we meet our most profound mentors and have the most transformative insights. While the Lower World is beautiful, strange, it is also scary. Unfamiliar and powerful creatures exist there and when visiting the realm, we must be on our guard not to be trapped or contaminated.

The Middle World is the energetic and observational analogue of our physical world. In this world of reality, we exist closest to ourselves yet a copy of ourselves which struggles and manages the

---

104

105 Wikipedia, "Soul."

106 themystica.com, "Altered States of Consciousness."

same issues as we do. Remote viewing, seeing, visiting and projections are all conducted mainly in the Middle World.

The Upper World is the realm of Spirit; Spirit is used here not spirits in multiple, although this is where they dwell too. It is an ethereal place which may have made some people think of a heaven. Often, we find teachers here, with important messages for the seeker or sick individual. Journeys to the Upper World often take place in contact with spirit guides, ancestors and sentient spirits.

While the shaman may visit and collect information from upper, lower, and middle worlds, they must understand the magnificence of the worlds they are visiting and what they are collecting from each for healing. Above all, they must not confuse or misapply what it is they have collected during a ritual.

Different methods are used to induce trances cross-culturally. These methods can require excessive physical movement including meditation, shamanic drumming, and dancing but may also involve sleep deprivation, fasting, sleep, and psychoactive drugs. These types of behaviours are not haphazard; if sleep deprivation is present, fasting and social isolation are often also present, such as when a young person goes alone into the forest on a quest for a guardian spirit. These types of induction methods rarely are associated with possession trance. [107]

If sleeping is the method to induce a trance usually it does not involve possession, such as a soul journey. Possession trances are associated with subsequent amnesia, convulsions, and spontaneous onset of trances. [108]

Trance and other altered states of consciousness are strongly associated with healing practices of shamans who are a subset of magico-religious healers. Among shamans, trances are usually induced by mechanisms such as singing, chanting, drumming, or dancing, after which the shaman in training or practice collapses and becomes unconscious and has intense visual experiences. These experiences presumably induce a state of relaxation that replaces fast brain activity in the front areas of the brain with slow wave activity representing more emotional information. [109]

Shamanic music[110] is music played either by actual shamans as part of their rituals, or by people who, whilst not themselves shamans, wish to evoke the cultural background of shamanism. So shamanic music includes both music used as part of shamans' rituals and music that refers to, or draws on, this.

In shamanism the shaman has a more active musical role than the medium in spirit possession. Although shamans use singing, drumming, and sometimes other instruments, a shamanic ritual is not a musical performance in the normal sense, and the music is directed more to spirits than to an audience and this shapes its musical dimension. A shaman uses various ways of making sounds to which different ritual purposes are ascribed. Of particular importance are the shaman's song and shaman's drumming.

_____

[107] Ibid.

[108] Ibid.

[109] https://hraf.yale.edu, "Altered States of Consciousness."
[110] Wikipedia, "Shamanic Music."

Siberian music groups drawing on a knowledge of shamanic culture have emerged. In the West shamanism has served as an imagined background to music meant to alter a listener's state of mind.

Korea and Tibet are two cultures where the music of shamanic ritual has interacted closely with other traditions.

How ritual forms the musical expression:

1. A shamanic ritual performance is, above all, a series of actions and not a series of musical sounds.

2. The intention of the shaman's actions and music are directed inwards towards his or her visualization of the spirit world and communicating with the spirits, and not outwards to any listeners who might be present.

3. Success of the ritual and its purpose in healing is clearly defined and differs greatly from, and ignores, any thought of performing entertainment.

4. Theatrical elements that have been added to impress an audience are of a type to make the contact with the spirits seem more real. They do not bear the performer's musical virtuosity. The added theatrical elements do not change the fundamental core of the shaman's ritual connection with the spirits must, and does, remain unchanged.

5. The overarching pace and tone and style of the music and singing proceeds at the pace of the spirits being communicated and the essential healing process being carried out. Theatrical considerations are ignored.

6. The rhythmic dimension of the music of shamans' rituals has been connected to the idea of both incorporating the rhythms of nature and magically rearticulating them.

Shamans in Tibet, Mongolia, and Northern Siberia are often skilled at working with plants and sacred herbs in order to provide or prescribe plant-based medicines for the recipient. Drumming, singing and dance are the usual ways for a shaman to induce an altered state of consciousness or trance state where they can journey to the spirit world and interact with their helping spirits and conduct spiritual healing. From time to time and depending on the shaman's lineage and method of practice, plants that have a psychoactive substance may induce a trance.

When using psychoactive substances, the shaman must be very careful because the substance is changing their state of consciousness and they do not control the intensity, duration and any residue left in their system once ingested. This is very different from a shaman using drumming, song, and dance where no drug is used. The shaman actively enters the spirit world and works with their helping spirits to perform their healing activity. They negotiate with her or his own helper spirit and then with other spirits as necessary, and moves between different territories of the upper middle and lower spirit worlds.

Whilst in the spirit world, the shaman must use considerable mental and spiritual awareness, they must be active and be able to take the initiative, a drug will impede their abilities and may make them susceptible to attack and damage by evil and malevolent spirits.

In contrast a medium is passive and possessed by the spirit or god, they are connected to and this results in a different musical style. Possession music is typically long in duration, mesmeric, loud and intense, with climaxes of rhythmic intensity and volume to which the medium has learned to respond by entering a trance state: the music is not played by the medium but by one or more musicians.[111]

In shamanism, the music is played by the shaman, the words in the song confirm the shaman's power, and is used actively by the shaman to modulate movements and changes of state as part of an active journey within the spirit world. In both cases the connection between music and an altered state of mind depends on both psychoacoustic and cultural factors, and the music cannot be said to cause' trance states.

It has been suggested that the drumming and singing of the shaman constitutes a system of sounds. This would suggest a system of semiotics shared between the shaman and the surrounding community. However, research suggests that if such a language exists, it is only understood by the shaman, other shaman, and the spirits being contacted, not the human community witnessing the ritual.

A shaman may use different sounds for different ritual purposes:

---

[111] Ibid.

11.1 Shaman's Drum

The single-headed frame drum is widely used in shamanic ritual, often with metallic ritual objects dangling inside, held by an interior wooden cross-piece, and played with a special beater that may also itself be a rattle.

The drum and rattle are made of specially chosen and consecrated materials. Wood from a tree felled by lightning, the skin from a particular animal, a drum beater that may also be a ritual rattle in it is own right. Finally, enlivened by the shaman's helping spirits. Enlivening means the drum will contain a particular spirit with whom the shaman maintains a relationship and the spirit will play a part in any rituals performed using it.

A number of theories have been advanced to explain the importance of percussion in ritual music in general. One line of explanation is psychoacoustic, whereby the tempo of the drum enables the shaman to enter the desired brain wave state, which corresponds to the number of beats per second of the drum.[112]

In shamanism a portable drum is better suited as it can be played easily and during rituals where the shaman must drum and dance. For this reason, the drumming is not restricted to regular tempo but may speed up and slow down with irregular accents. In some regions, the skin of a shaman's drum should be cut after his/her death. This allows the spirit enlivening the drum to be released, and so that no other shaman, or ordinary person, can use the drum to connect with the spirit world using it.

The drumbeat acts like a tether for the journeyer to hold onto as they travel and it keeps them grounded. Let's use the example of a kite. The kite is the person who is journeying. The string is the sound of the drum. Live drumming induces a deeper ASC as it also usually involves dance and physical motion.

---

[112] Ibid.

11.2 Bon Shamanic Music and Buddhism

Bon predates Tibetan Buddhism. When Buddhism arrived in approximately the eigh[th] century AD, both religions began competing with each other, but they also incorporated many of each other's practices. The Bön shaman's drum, but now placed on a pole became part of Tibetan Buddhist ritual music ensembles. The Shang—a kind of bell cymbal—became incorporated in Buddhist rituals.[113] It was formerly only used by shamans to clear away negative energy before shamanic rituals. [114]

The Shang bell is not the same as the Tibetan Buddhist Tingsha bell.

The practice of giving a sonorous identity to deities, of calling them and sending them back by means of sounds, may well have entered Tibetan Buddhist ritual from Bön tradition. [115]

11.3 Bells and Cymbals

Bells and symbols are used in conjunction with the drum as part of the ritual and are essential to the safety of the shaman as they enter an altered state of consciousness and exist in the spirit world.

Bells and symbols are used for purifying the ritual space. This is because a ritual involving contact with the spirits is always potentially dangerous, and one of the dangers is that of pollution.

Bells and cymbals may be attached to the shamans' costume, the drum and drum better or rattle they are using to ensure safety and purification of all clothing and ensure the sound created by the shaman is purified. Sound can also be used as a healing power, conceived as a way of directing spiritual energy from the shaman into an afflicted person. In Tuva sick people are said to have been healed by the sound of a stringed instrument made from a tree struck by lightning.[116]

11.4 Shaman Dreams

Dreaming, a nearly universal channel into an altered state of consciousness, and is much more widely available than lengthy rituals with music and dance or use of drugs.

A shaman will use their own dreams and the dreams of the person they are to heal as part of the divination and diagnosis process to determine how to proceed. At the end of the ritual and after a period of healing, use of dreams by the Shaman can confirm success of the rituals and healing or whether further intervention is required.

Figure 13. Tibetan Buddhist Ceremonial Drum

11.5 Other   Thoughts

---

[113] https://garudashop.com/collections/bonpo-shang-bell, "Bonpo Shang Bell | Traditional Tibetan Instrument."
[114] Wikipedia, "Shamanic Music."
[115] Ibid.
[116] Ibid.

Other cultures say that it is the patient that must achieve the trance, not the shaman. In Islamic North Africa and the Arabian Peninsula, the zar ritual is used to rid negative spirits from the body of the patient, but the leader of the ceremony does not go into trance, it is the patient that must achieve ecstasy for healing to occur. In A'isha Ali's video of "Dances of Egypt" she shows a zar ceremony, and music and dance are essential for the patient to achieve trance. While there is definitely a leader of the ceremony, a shaman figure, she is merely the orchestrator/mediator of the event, not the central figure. [117]

---

[117] KatyaFaris.com, "Altered States of Consciousness and Healing in Indigenous Rituals – Katya Faris."

12   Appendix a: The Shaman Podcast—Reincarnation

The following is the show notes for Episode 2 of the Shaman Podcast where we had a short discussion on Reincarnation.

Speaker —   Mark A. Ashford
               Usui Tibetan Reiki Master and Teacher

What this is—Hello and welcome to the "The Shaman Podcast."

What we talk about in this Podcast —

- Shamanism

- Reiki—Reiki energy healing, especially the lineage I follow originated in Tibet, in Shamanistic practices that were recorded in Tibetan Buddhist Texts and practices from the eigh[th] century onward.

Media —

- This Podcast is one of several media available to you to help you understand and develop your awareness of energy healing and practices, history, tradition and a little anthropology.

The others are

- YouTube videos — "Reiki with Candice, Mark, and Opame"—Candice and Opame are two of my guides.

- Books—eBooks and Paperback books—in full colour available on Amazon.ca

- Online courses at Teachable.com

- A blog at ThePracticalShaman.ca

Today we are talking about: Reincarnation

Reincarnation is the philosophical or religious concept that the non-physical essence of a living being, its soul or Spirit starts a new life in a different physical form or body after biological death. It is also called rebirth, transmigration or metempsychosis.

Reincarnation is a central tenet of the main Indian religions; Jainism, Buddhism, Sikhism and Hinduism. Some Hindu groups that do not believe in reincarnation, instead they believe in an afterlife.

It is found in many streams of orthodox Judaism as well as some North American Natives and some Native Australians.

Historic Greek figures, such as Pythagoras, Socrates, and Plato all believed in and wrote about reincarnation.

The Celts and Druids had a central core belief that the soul does not die. After death it passes from one body into another … the main object for this is education. The soul learns or relearns about existence from one life to another but itself is indestructible.

Taoist beliefs as far back as the Han Dynasty 206 BC—AD 220 describe reincarnation as "Birth is not a beginning; death is not an end. There is existence without limitation; there is continuity without a starting point."

The majority of the major sects in Christianity and Islam do not believe in reincarnation, but some such as the Cathars, Alawites, Druze, and the Rosicrucians do.

It is the doctrine of salvation in Christianity that prevents belief in reincarnation. Islam believes in a linear life at the end of which a person is judged and sent either to Hell or Heaven. On judgment day all are resurrected.

Personally, I think of my body as a container, a container in which my soul exists and is able to experience the physical world. Through each lifetime, my soul learns lessons about existence and balances its Karma, and in so doing, it becomes enlightened. When it achieves enlightenment, it breaks free of this plane of existence and has a choice to move on, or, continue but on its terms. When a particular spirit is so moved by compassion and love for those of us still in the throes of birthing pains again and again, it comes back to teach and heal.

The intermediate or transitional state between death and reincarnation is known as the Bardo in Buddhism. It is in this state that Near-Death Experiences [NDE] are recorded.

It is at this time, after death and before rebirth that the shaman plays his/her most important role.

A soul or spirit may not immediately be reincarnated to the next physical form. The soul may not accept the death of their physical body, which may have ended because of an accident, sudden illness or even violence. The soul may linger in the current world as a non-physical essence and attach themselves to a physical person such as a loved one or a completely unrelated individual. This may hurt or damage the physical person they have attached to. Damage manifests as illness.

Shamans operate primarily within the spiritual world, which they believe affects the human world. A Shaman healing the soul or spirit of a living person restores their physical body to balance and wholeness.

In so doing, the Shaman encounters the source of the sickness, the attached soul that has not passed over to be reincarnated and guides it to the spirit world where it can manifest into a new physical being, healed and capable of continuing on their journey.

In other situations, relatives may engage a shaman to seek out the soul of the deceased and help it cross over and reincarnate normally.

I hope this podcast has been informative and interesting. Please, subscribe to the Podcast so receive future episodes, and check out our other materials to help in understanding Shamanism, Reiki and energy healing.

I look forward to seeing you in the next Episode.

Bye for now.

Bibliography:

Bibleinfo.com. "What Is the Fruit of the Spirit?".
Britannica. "Bardo ThöDol Tibetan Buddhist Text."
Collection, University of California Press eBook. "The Spiritual Quest." (1982 - 2004).
Dictionary, Merriam-Webster. "Definition of Soul by Merriam-Webster."
Dictionary.com. "Near-Death Experience | Definition of near-Death Experience."
Encyclopedia, Chinese Buddhist. "Eight Classes of Gods and Demons."
G N M Tyrrell, H H Price. "Apparitions 1953.Pdf."
Gaia. "What Is Astral Projection? An Astral Projecting Guide.Pdf."
GotQuestions.org. "What Is the Difference between the Soul and Spirit of Man?".
HowStuffWorks. "What Is Going on during a near-Death Experience?".
http://donlehmanjr.com/. "The Tibetan Book of the Dead.Pdf."
http://healerofheartsandminds.com. "Reincarnation, Past Lives, Suffering and the Bible, a
        Shaman's Views."
https://garudashop.com/collections/bonpo-shang-bell. "Bonpo Shang Bell | Traditional
        Tibetan Instrument."
https://hraf.yale.edu. "Altered States of Consciousness."
https://lissarankin.com, Lissa Rankin. "20 Diagnostic Signs That You're Suffering from Soul
        Loss."
https://www.energy-shifter.com/shamanism-and-spiritual-techniques.html. "Shamanism, and
        Soul Retrieval - Spiritual House Cleansing."
https://www.wisdomlib.org. "Antarabhava, AntarāBhava 2 Definitions."
KatyaFaris.com. "Altered States of Consciousness and Healing in Indigenous Rituals – Katya
        Faris."
Lionsroar.com. "The Four Points of Letting Go in the Bardo."
Philosophy, Stanford Encyclopedia of. "Descartes and the Pineal Gland."
RationalWiki. "Near-Death Experience."
Rinpoche, Tenzin Wangyal. "Soul Retrieval and Related Ideas."
———. "Tibetan Soul Retrieval."
Theinnervoyage.com. "Soul Retrieval."
themystica.com. "Altered States of Consciousness."
wanttoknow.info. "Remote Viewing.Pdf."
Wiki, Rigpa. "Eight Classes of Gods and Demons."
Wikipeda. "Bernard Lonergan."
———. "History of the Location of the Soul."
———. "Oswald Spengler."
Wikipedia. "Bardo."
———. "Bardo Thodol."
———. "Carl Jung."
———. "Carol Zaleski."
———. "Celia Green.Pdf."
———. "Daniel A. Helminiak."
———. "Dissociation Psychology."
———. "Ensoulment."
———. "Holy Spirit."
———. "Human Spirit."
———. "New Age."
———. "Out-of-Body Experience."

———. "Reincarnation."
———. "Remote Viewing.Pdf."
———. "Robert Monroe.Pdf."
———. "Shamanic Music."
———. "Skandha."
———. "Sogyal Rinpoche."
———. "Soul."
———. "Spirit."
———. "Spirit - Wikipedia."
———. "Terton."
———. "Thomas Aquinas."
Woolger, Dr. Roger J. "Beyond Death- Transition and the Afterlife."
www.rigpawiki.org. "Emptiness."
———. "Nyingma Buddhism."

Bibliography:

Bibleinfo.com. "What Is the Fruit of the Spirit?".
Britannica. "Bardo ThöDol Tibetan Buddhist Text."
Collection, University of California Press eBook. "The Spiritual Quest." (1982 - 2004).
Dictionary, Merriam-Webster. "Definition of Soul by Merriam-Webster."
Dictionary.com. "Near-Death Experience | Definition of near-Death Experience."
Encyclopedia, Chinese Buddhist. "Eight Classes of Gods and Demons."
G N M Tyrrell, H H Price. "Apparitions 1953.Pdf."
Gaia. "What Is Astral Projection? An Astral Projecting Guide.Pdf."
GotQuestions.org. "What Is the Difference between the Soul and Spirit of Man?".
HowStuffWorks. "What Is Going on during a near-Death Experience?".
http://donlehmanjr.com/. "The Tibetan Book of the Dead.Pdf."
http://healerofheartsandminds.com. "Reincarnation, Past Lives, Suffering and the Bible, a Shaman's Views."
https://garudashop.com/collections/bonpo-shang-bell. "Bonpo Shang Bell | Traditional Tibetan Instrument."
https://hraf.yale.edu. "Altered States of Consciousness."
https://lissarankin.com, Lissa Rankin. "20 Diagnostic Signs That You're Suffering from Soul Loss."
https://www.energy-shifter.com/shamanism-and-spiritual-techniques.html. "Shamanism, and Soul Retrieval - Spiritual House Cleansing."
https://www.wisdomlib.org. "Antarabhava, AntarāBhava 2 Definitions."
KatyaFaris.com. "Altered States of Consciousness and Healing in Indigenous Rituals – Katya Faris."
Lionsroar.com. "The Four Points of Letting Go in the Bardo."
Philosophy, Stanford Encyclopedia of. "Descartes and the Pineal Gland."
RationalWiki. "Near-Death Experience."
Rinpoche, Tenzin Wangyal. "Soul Retrieval and Related Ideas."
———. "Tibetan Soul Retrieval."
Theinnervoyage.com. "Soul Retrieval."
themystica.com. "Altered States of Consciousness."
wanttoknow.info. "Remote Viewing.Pdf."

Wiki, Rigpa. "Eight Classes of Gods and Demons."
Wikipeda. "Bernard Lonergan."
———. "History of the Location of the Soul."
———. "Oswald Spengler."
Wikipedia. "Bardo."
———. "Bardo Thodol."
———. "Carl Jung."
———. "Carol Zaleski."
———. "Celia Green.Pdf."
———. "Daniel A. Helminiak."
———. "Dissociation Psychology."
———. "Ensoulment."
———. "Holy Spirit."
———. "Human Spirit."
———. "New Age."
———. "Out-of-Body Experience."
———. "Reincarnation."
———. "Remote Viewing.Pdf."
———. "Robert Monroe.Pdf."
———. "Shamanic Music."
———. "Skandha."
———. "Sogyal Rinpoche."
———. "Soul."
———. "Spirit."
———. "Spirit - Wikipedia."
———. "Terton."
———. "Thomas Aquinas."
Woolger, Dr. Roger J. "Beyond Death- Transition and the Afterlife."
www.rigpawiki.org. "Emptiness."
———. "Nyingma Buddhism."